It Happened in WOODSTOCK

STONECROP

Library of Congress Catalog Card Number 77-172442
Copyright © 1972 by Stonecrop

All rights reserved under
International and Pan-American
Copyright Laws

STONECROP
WOODSTOCK, N. Y.
NEW YORK   LONDON

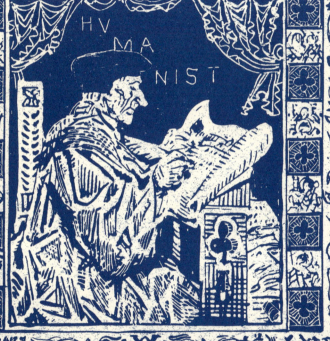

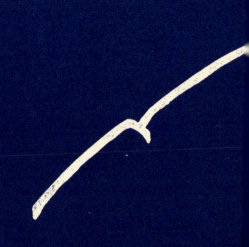

WOODSTOCK:

CONTENTS

WOODSTOCK:	A Foreword	xi
WOODSTOCK:	A Fourth Dimensional View A Chronological Study	3
WOODSTOCK:	It Happened in The Saga of Woodstock	31
WOODSTOCK:	A Nostalgic Portrait The Woodstock Maverick Festival of 1915	133
WOODSTOCK:	A Psychic Portrait The Woodstock Music Festival of 1969	141
WOODSTOCK:	An Addendum	153
	Credits	163

ix

Woodstock—in the shadow of Overlook Mountain

WOODSTOCK: A Foreword

"Woodstock! ... it is a unique spot in the world, isn't it? Throbbing with creation, flashing with genius—and so placid and countrified withal."

> —Helen Hayes, an actress who played in summer stock at the village's Maverick Theatre.

"Anyone who knows Woodstock will agree, I think, that it is a charming place. It shows what good taste and imagination can do to create a delightful atmosphere."

> —Mrs. Franklin D. Roosevelt, "columnist," who wrote up her visit to Woodstock in "My Day," a nationally syndicated feature.

"The only ladders in Woodstock are the ones we pull up to keep people away...."

> —Mrs. Birge Harrison, wife of the well-known painter who led, for many years, the summer classes of the Art Students League in Woodstock.

The story of Woodstock—a community heralded in recent years as progenitor of a Nation, an entire Generation—was first recorded by Anita M. Smith in her *Woodstock: History and Hearsay*.

An "impression of braided suit worn by Miss Anita Smith" which appeared in a 1911 issue of Philadelphia's *The Evening Bulletin*

Miss Smith, a refugee of Philadelphia's *crème de la crème* (she had made her debut as one of the exalted Inner Assembly—and then rebelled, coming to Woodstock with money intended for a ball gown) joined the village's fledgling Artists Colony in the summer of 1912. As painter, then writer and herbalist, she mentally assimilated the myriad legends and records which document the phenomenon that is Woodstock.

This book, *It Happened in Woodstock,* an abridged and updated version of the story which emerged,* draws the body of its text at least partly from that source. But this edition includes as well a "fourth dimensional view" —a kind of chronological study. (In metaphysical circles the fourth dimension is generally agreed to embody "crystallized time sequences" or photographically-preserved events. In other words, it is perfectly possible to "travel back" and rewitness history as it actually occurred.)

It Happened in Woodstock offers, too, an account of the much-publicized Woodstock Music Festival of August, 1969.** Placed at the end of the book, this will be viewed, it is hoped in its proper perspective—as simply one of the more recent of a continuing series of festivals associated with Woodstock. (The village has long been suspected of honoring Pan

A young artist's* arrival in Woodstock

*A.M.S.

as one of its patron dieties, so well established is this tradition of the music fête.) The division-title, "Woodstock: A Psychic Portrait," is evidential of the intuitive ideal sought in recounting the event—one seemingly cataclysmic when taken in itself; and yet, hardly so monumental when witnessed as merely another chapter of the continuing saga of Woodstock.

---

* *Woodstock, History and Hearsay*, now available in its second printing, as a Stonecrop Publication
** Ironically enough, this Festival did, in fact, take place sixty miles to the south and west.

EDITORS' APOLOGY

We, as Piceans, have been in error. The reader will note that the attitude taken toward the Woodstock Music Festival of 1969 is, in all but the final section of this book, one of unmerited condescension. For it was our purpose, as stated above, to place this festival into the context of the history of Woodstock itself. We felt that the event had been blown—through some vagary of the public mind—out of all proper historical proportion.

But we have since concluded—with the persuasion of our London observer—that public attention, in this case at least, has been anything but arbitrary.

The "happening" of August, 1969 *is* a part of the village of Woodstock. But of far more importance has been its *Cosmic* role.

It Happened
in
WOODSTOCK

WOODSTOCK: A Fourth Dimensional View

B.C.   Soon—comparatively speaking—after the Coming of Light, the Indian god Manitou sends down from the sky the first woman, in the shape of a tortoise. (We may assume that Man was to follow shortly, in the form of a child-tortoise. Or perhaps as a piece of the lady's shell. . . .)

A.D. 1614   The first map of the Hudson River Valley is made to be sent to Holland. "Woodstock," a name of Saxon derivation, is obviously missing.

1777   The Englishman, Robert Livingston, mentions Woodstock in a letter. It is by this time, as we may gather from one of his remarks, a thoroughly established settlement. The original Saxon word was "Wudestoc," for "a clearing in the wood." This village in New York doubtless borrowed its appellation from the (woodsy) town in Oxfordshire, England.

1806   The Woodstock Glass Manufacturing Society produces a viable window pane. For many persons not engaged in this, or subsequent glass-

making ventures, the Tannery in Woodstock provides a welcome recourse from unemployment.

1845 John Lasher, agent for a tax-collector, is assisted into his tar-filled boots as part of the farmers' rebellion of the "Down Rent War."

1874 James T. Shotwell, future historian and international mediator (to the French, a usually cynical people, he was actually "the great American leader for peace"), is born in Canada, destined to become a most distinguished citizen of Woodstock— and *par extension*, the world.

1880 Ralph Radcliffe Whitehead (a founder-to-be of the Woodstock Artists Colony) receives his Master of Arts degree at Balliol College, Oxford. Having been influenced by socialist theories of the day, and deploring the de-humanization apparent in the English factory system, he is already planning his "ideal community"*; one of various craftsmen, each dedicated to the creation of beautiful objects, while in an atmosphere healthful to mind and body alike.

---

* This project was later to be carried out at Byrdcliffe. (See map.)

Some "nest-ees" of the super-club at Byrdcliffe ... including Lucy Brown (second from left), married to one of the Colony founders, and a Mr. Erlandson (seated), head cabinet-maker for Woodstock's "ideal community"

1902   The "Larks' Nest" or super-club is formed at Byrdcliffe. Its conceptual purpose—to serve as common, habitational ground for a *variety* of intellectual viewpoints—is so successful that it is quickly renamed the "Wasps' Nest."

c.1905   Albert Webster, engineer, architect, and resident of Byrdcliffe, sets up a Christmas tree for the neighboring birds. When the birds ignore it, disappointing the Webster children, Albert dons a feather duster and hops about, taking pecks at seed

affixed to the branches. The children react with whoops of joy, but a sudden visitor (from the stuffy, outside world) registers shock and disbelief.

1906 The Art Students League of New York City establishes its summer home in Woodstock. The surrounding mountains are soon bespeckled with platoons of enthusiastic fledglings, bearing canvases, palettes, brushes, and multi-colored umbrellas. One old lady habitually trundles her gear in a baby carriage.

Umbrella-ed instruction for a member of the Art Students League

1915 The first Woodstock Festival occurs on the Maverick. Staged to defray the cost of a much-needed artesian well, it is repeated in successive seasons to pay off the innumerable creditors of the Maverick himself, Hervey White.

1916 A concert hall* is opened on the Maverick, providing the villagers with Sunday recitals of chamber music. Everyone is welcomed — even the pets and babies. And admission is free—unless one opts for the comfort of a freshly hewn plank, which is offered at a cost of twenty-five cents.

1919 An Art Association is founded, with a board of directors equally representing the academic and radical groups. When in 1920 the Association has acquired its own studio and the board is selecting the paintings to appear in a forthcoming exhibition, a "conservative" becomes ill and is forced to leave. One of the radicals gallantly offers to take his place. As each painting is presented, he casts two votes—one against, the other, for.

---
* This hall was built from surrounding trees; long poles were used for the frame, with rough boards added for the roof and sides.

The studio or gallery of the Woodstock Art Association

1924 The Maverick Theatre makes its pyrotechnical debut with *The Dragon*, by Lady Gregory. The star-studded cast (Helen Hayes, Edward G. Robinson, *et al.*) plays through a cloud of clay dust to an audience seated on the open hill.

1937 The Woodstock Playhouse is completed, and the Colony's theatrical impulse — which had gradually dwindled on the Maverick*—is re-

---

* The Loft Players, one of the last groups to perform under the aegis of Hervey White, had moved to the Greenwich Village "Circle-in-the-Square," and with spectacular success, virtually initiated the entire "off-Broadway" phenomenon.

stored to its former grandeur. A gala performance in 1941 (staged in support of the France Forever movement) features a string-quartet playing Debussey, ballet dancers from the Paris Opera, a Degas Tableau, des chansons populaires, and of course, the Marseillaise. . . .

1938 *The Phoenix* springs from the ashes of *The Wild Hawk, The Plowshare, The Hue and Cry,*** *The Woodstock Bulletin, The Saturday Morning,* and other periodicals, all devoted to the essays, poems, reviews, fiction, and woodcuts of the "local" artists. . . . In its first issue, *The Phoenix* prints a remarkable essay by D. H. Lawrence (a piece probably secured through the efforts of Henry Miller, the quarterly's European editor) in which Mr. Lawrence proclaims that ". . . still in America, among the Indians, the oldest Pan is alive. . . ." This is indeed a fitting introduction for a publication born on the Maverick—a place attuned to the spirit of Pan, and echoing that of the American Indian.

** This was, according to one description, "printed on pages of two colors which changed weekly, as did the pen name of one of its columnists."

THE PHŒNIX

A QUARTERLY

Vol. I No. I.   Spring 1938

A flight from the ashes

The home of the Woodstock Guild of Craftsmen—as it looked just before the turn of the century . . . It is said that General Ulysses Grant once spent a night here before continuing up the mountain—where his name appears in the Mead House register of guests.

1940 The Woodstock Guild of Craftsmen, Inc. is founded by a group of weavers, potters, woodcarvers and jewelry workers as a small co-operative enterprise. In 1945, an attractive home on the Village Green is acquired for the organization. (It is the same property which had once belonged to William Deforest —whose ownership was marred, however, by the controversy resulting from his building a private (privy) plumbing housure four inches onto the land of the neighboring Coons.) The Guild is destined to grow and flourish for at least the following thirty-one years.

1941 Woodstock mobilizes in support of France Forever, a cause initiated after the collapse of France in the Second World War, and designed to promote resistance. The (inevitable) series of festivals, concerts, films and lectures are subsequently sponsored, through which a considable sum is raised. In the years after, fund drives of this sort are also held for Britain, Russia, and many of the smaller Allied Nations.

A poster for a France Forever fund-raising dance scheduled on Bastille Day

In 1953, Archduke Rodolph—son of the late Emperor Ferdinand of Austria—and his bride, Xenia Czernichev-Besobrasov, spent their honeymoon in Hickory Hollow (at the base of Overlook; see map) following the wedding service (above) at which Bishop Fulton Sheen presided. When another member of European royalty, ex-King Peter of Yugoslavia, also visited Woodstock, he stayed further up Overlook Mountain.

c.1954 The Woodstock Artists Association, having previously held several art conferences of national scope, now organizes the first International Art Film Festival. The "Seventh Lively Art" is thus officially launched in the Colony.

1956 The Turnau Opera Company converts the old Byrdcliffe "library" (originally used as such by Whitehead's craftsmen-intellectuals, and later as a theatre by the Phoenix—and other—Players) into a tiny but effective opera house and by the 1958 Summer Season is able to boast performances of twenty-one different operas, including four world premières of contemporary American works.

1960 The Playhouse institutes a special program of musical presentation, sponsoring top performers in the fields of Folk, Rock, Jazz and Blues—perhaps to complement the Maverick concerts featuring more classical types of music.

1969 A Woodstock Music Festival is polarized at White Lake, N. Y.—sixty miles from the village of Woodstock. It constitutes, "for three days of peace and music," a veritable metropolis—third largest in New

Turnau Opera Association, Inc.
presents

T. O. P.

TURNAU OPERA PLAYERS
BYRDCLIFFE THEATRE
Woodstock, N. Y.

July 4 - September 1, 1958

Performances Fridays, Saturdays, Tuesdays and Wednesdays at 8:30 p.m.

A program cover for the TOP performances of 1958

Hervey White reclining on one of the more comfortable "planks" in front of his Maverick Concert Hall

York State, with a population of approximately 400,000.

1971 The Maverick Concert Hall — as originally built by Hervey White — opens for its fifty-sixth consecutive season of music. (This chamber music series is now the oldest program of its kind existing anywhere in the country.) Unfortunately, a welcome is no longer extended to pets and babies. . . .

WOODSTOCK: It Happened in

> There's a patch of moss on a hillside,
>   With a sheltering tree above.
> 'Twas only these and a casual cloud
>   Saw how I loved my Love.
>
> Or maybe that quaint cicada
>   Somewhere high on a tree,
> Grew shrill with passion just because
>   He saw how my Love loved me.

So wrote the poet Shames O'Sheal in the early part of this century, entitling the piece, "It Happened in Woodstock." Woodstock has been many things to many different people. But for everyone, it has been something of a catalyst—things always *happen* in Woodstock.... Whether one attributes it to the iron in the mountains, to an underground river, or simply to Fate and historical coincidence, the fact remains immutable: Woodstock is, and has consistently been a place of unusual activity. But more important, it is a village of *inspired* momentum, of constructive and ever progressive evolution.

Woodstock ... something of a catalyst

The history of Woodstock does then, necessarily possess considerable charm and fascination.... Its narrative can be said to begin with the Indian god Manitou, for when the great sea subsided and the Catskill Mountains emerged, it was he who sent down from the sky the first woman, in the shape of a tortoise. She became the ancestor of the Mohicans, who later lived behind the ramparts of the Wall of Manitou, several thousand feet above the Hudson River Valley.

Manitou himself was thought to have lived on Overlook Mountain, and the Indians were careful never to stray too close, lest they incite his wrath. Then too, the mountain exerted a drag upon their footsteps. When on long

marches, if they happened to pass nearby, they found it necessary to camp for a while—continuing their journey only when they had mustered the strength to counteract the mountain's pull.

Many years later, this land was sold to Johannes Hardenburgh by Indian Chief Nanisonus, who signed the deed with his mark of a tortoise. But even today it is not unusual to hear of people coming to Woodstock—the village at the foot of Overlook Mountain—and staying weeks, months, often years, before they are able at last to tear themselves away...

Perhaps the oldest inhabitant of Woodstock is an ancient squaw who is thought to live on in the mountain, controlling the thus vituperative weather. For there is a stream running down from Overlook which sometimes becomes a snarling torrent, ravaging the countryside on its path into the village. It would seem to be the squaw who, angry with us for destroying the trees in our continual efforts to expand the village, sends these storms to wash us from her hills and valleys.

The Spirit of the American Indian is firmly established in our mountains, and we find in our daily lives constant reminders of its presence. Several very tangible (and thus superficial) examples are the Indian names we still employ—for the Onteoras, Ohayo Mountain.

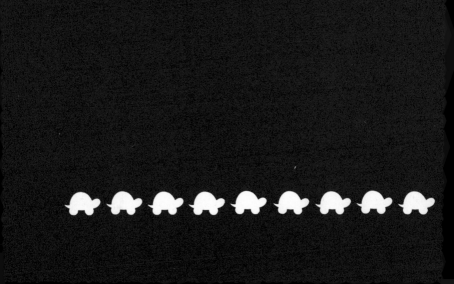

Overlook . . . peaceful enough at a distance . . . but it's springtime, the snows are melting, and the old squaw is seasonably crotchety

and the Esopus River; the beads, pipes and leather goods, or so-called "Hippie" affectations abundant in the village; and even the arrowheads and bits of broken pottery occasionally overturned in gardening, drilling, or blasting.

Relics from a much later epoch occasionally discovered through these latter processes are the fragments of glass and chards dating from the years of glass manufacture in the early nineteenth century. This, the first organized industry of the white man in Woodstock Township, was in accordance with the tradition of handicraft and creativity initiated by the Indians, and later carried on by denizens of the Artists Colony. For along with the usual window panes were made some very beautiful pieces—including glass pitchers, domes, canes,

and birds. But even more interesting to us today are the records left by the Woodstock Glass Manufacturing Society and the later Bristol Company.

From this Company's store account—for the workers were often paid in store goods, rather than direct and useless wages—it is evident that glassblowers were rather extravagant in taste as well as dress. Several, we read, preferred—and could afford—wine or brandy instead of the usual rum. Augustus Greele is known to have purchased forty-three yards of French Shirting; Conrad Lister bought *"muslin de laine"* for the Hasbrouck girl and silk handkerchiefs for himself—a half dozen at a time. John G. Evans, a master blower, indulged in seven yards of bombazette, and many lengths of ribbons. Others, buying glazed cotton, alpaca, palmetto and cashmere, were all more fortunate than the lowly pair who each bought "half a hat."

Stories of the glamorous blowers understandably persisted for many years. A Mrs. Loretta Short of Wittenberg recalled that they "made big money and threw it around." They

A lovely, blown glass pitcher made by one of the tonier dressers

were "real tony dressers" and dazzled the women with their embroidered waistcoats. They made far more than ordinary farm boys, whose most extravagant ornamentation, we may gather from a notice in the Kingston Sentinel, might be the bottle green of a surtout coat, or the neutral shade of linsey-woolsey pantaloons.

From another item in that local paper we infer what other histories have often told us— that the lot of women was, in those days, unenviable. One ad states: "My wife Polly has left my bed and board for no good reason." Or so he says ... "As she is fond of riding, I forbid anyone to pick her up in a sleigh, carriage or wheelbarrow." Poor Polly, not allowed even a whirl in a wheelbarrow!

Surfeited with similar injustice, some of the women turned early to the cause of feminism. One such stalwart was Betty Booth Macdaniels:

"I was the first woman to go on record for wearin' trousers in Woodstock, seein' as how I picked wild strawberries in my husband's breeches—a darin' thing to do!"

She was known as a vigorous walker:

"Why I thought nothing of trampin' to Saugerties or Kingston (a distance of ten miles) an' comin' home with a bag of meal on my back! An' if it was cold—why I just took a steamin' brick or two."

She was best known for her skill at doctoring:

"They'd all come to me an' say I've got this wrong or that aches—A'nt Betsy, what can yer do for me?"

She gathered herbs and made infusions, such as sweet fern for fever, spearmint for stomach ache, catnip for jumpy nerves, gentian —called blue blows stuff—for dysentery. But best known of all was her syrup of sassafras for coughs.

"My three sons were soldiers in the Civil War and they would write home askin' for it. So I'd stay up all night to watch my crocks of syrup on the back of the stove and then send it off by the caseload."

A lady from Willow, who concocted similar remedies, mentioned also an onion syrup for colds.

"An' arbutus was known as gravel weed because of its use for kidney troubles. We never thought of it for a flower."

Among the wild flowers in the Catskill Mountains, the Trailing Arbutus, often called May Flower, is one of the loveliest.

"There's not a weed that grows which isn't good for something."

She used pennyroyal for croup, and plantain leaves for her children's bruises.

"There's not a weed that grows which isn't good for something."

They would have taken a dim view of remedies such as "Trask's Magnetic Salve," "Pain-Killer," "Family Pills" and "Condition Powder," each readily available at the Bristol Company Store. But it is evident from store accounts that the glassblowers, at least, all trusted implicitly the curative powers of these sophisticated panaceas.

The glass companies flourished for a number of years, but in the 1840's business was slow, bills became ever more difficult to settle, and the era of glassmaking in the Woodstock Township was nearly at an end. This period is

Under the leadership of "Black Hawk" and "Big Thunder," the farmers of the Down Rent War rode forth in disguises of sheepskin masks and painted jerkins.

better remembered for unrest among the farmers, resulting in a number of uprisings collectively known as the Down Rent War. The systems of land leasing and patronship prevalent in New York had long been notoriously feudal; by the early forties, the farmers had been driven beyond endurance. Having failed by legal means to redress the injustices, they followed the example of their Boston compatriots by donning Indian disguises and setting out for a bit of tar and feathering. The actual violence

committed was laughably inconsequential; one of the greatest casualties was the sheriff whose hat was knocked from his head. But the songs composed and chanted during this period express the determination of the farmers:

THE END OF BIG BILL SNYDER

The moon was shining silver bright
When the sheriff came at dead of night;
High on the hill stood an Indian true,
And on his horn a blast he blew —

    Out of the way of big Bill Snyder,
    Out of the way of big Bill Snyder,
    Out of the way of big Bill Snyder,
        Tar his coat and feather his hide, Sir!

Bill thought he heard the sound of a gun;
And he cried in his fright, "My race is run!
Far better for me had I never been born,
Than to come to the sound of that tin horn!"

Bill ran and ran till he reached the wood,
And there in horror still he stood;
For he saw a savage, tall and grim,
And he heard a tin horn not a rod from him —

Next day the body of Bill was found;
His wits all scattered on the ground;
And by his side a jug of rum,
Which showed how Bill to his end had come.

    Out of the way of big Bill Snyder,
    Out of the way of big Bill Snyder,
    Out of the way of big Bill Snyder,
        Tar his coat and feather his hide, Sir!

This so called "war" was at least partially responsible for the subsequent abolishment of feudal tenures. As so often happens in Woodstock, the workers, the real doers, were triumphant in the end.

🐘🐘🐘🐘🐘🐘🐘

Ralph Radcliffe Whitehead, a founder of the artists colony in Woodstock, would have sympathized with the cause, for he deeply respected farmers, tradesmen and all those who lived by their hands. While studying at Oxford, he was greatly influenced by the Socialist ideals of Ruskin and William Morris. Much later, in

Ralph Radcliffe Whitehead, a founder of the Artists Colony in Woodstock, was deeply influenced by the Socialist ideals of Ruskin and William Morris.

1903, with his project at Byrdcliffe already underway, he wrote an article entitled "A Plea for Manual Work" in which he said:

"... the beauty and joy of life seems too often to be lost through the haste to get somewhere too quickly ... nature works slowly ... and the ties which bind us to her larger soul are torn and weakened by our impotent restlessness and love of novelty ... the joy of a man in the work of his hands is not a mere passing satisfaction, but is an element of sane life."

Byrdcliffe—taken from the middle names of himself and his wife, Jane Byrd Macall—was to be a working example of these precepts: he hoped to combine with a country life manual and intellectual activity. And he gave a welcome to any craftsman who was in sympathy with these ideas and would help to realize them.

Among the artists who came were woodworkers, bookbinders, potters, weavers, picture framers and even designers of furniture. Ned Thatcher, one of the several graduates of Pratt Institute who early joined the colony, was set to work making decorative hinges and locks for some of the Byrdcliffe chests and cupboards. He had a delightful sense of humor, and was clever at imitating the talk of the local farmers. He employed this talent to such advantage that eventually he was unable to speak in any other

Besides working on the Byrdcliffe furniture, Ned Thatcher (alias "Iddie Flitcher") held classes in metal craft.
Photograph by
Konrad Cramer

idiom. He wrote funny prose and poetry for the local paper, signing with the name of "Iddie Flitcher." One such piece is entitled "Winter," and in its ungrammatical style it has a kind of homely truth and beauty:

WINTER

It's a-snowin' pretty out an' litein' on the pines n' things
Even the old junk pile is kivered up 'till it looks like the icin' on a cake
It's one of them still days when you kin hear enjin whistles far off n' the trains a-roarin' down the track
This snow reminds me of the crullers ma used to make all thick with powdered sugar on the top
Pease an' quiet fer them that kin see an' hear it but these is few.

(Iddie Flitcher)

From the frantic pace of the far-off city . . .

... to "pease an' quiet for them that kin see an' hear it ..."
Snow-mantled Highways
Painting by John F. Carlson

One of the more luxurious Byrdcliffe studios

Marie Little, who lived in a Byrdcliffe studio she fondly called "The Cricket," was emphatically among the "few" whom "Mr. Flitcher" mentions. A weaver by trade, she turned out attractive mats, bags and curtains made from cotton strips. These she colored with natural dyes of barks and berries, which gave her materials the tones of the woods and fields. Her studio was a nut brown with accents of black and orange. The sparse furnishings and floors were always freshly cleaned and oiled.

In her youth she had studied music in Italy, where her poplar-like figure and quivering voice were admired. But as the seasons passed in Byrdcliffe, and no one was left who remembered her music, she withdrew more and more into herself. In this solitary life she vibrated to refinements that others could not perceive.

She did, however, extend occasional invitations to persons whom she hoped might savor the nuances of her esoteric ways. The guest was certain to be painfully conscious of his dusty footsteps on her carefully polished floors; he dared not move from the chair allotted him, for he knew he had undoubtedly been placed there to see the graceful branch of an apple tree against the mountain, or the lovely vista of the path up to a sumac.

Because she was so poor, she scorned what only wealth could buy. In contrast, she made a

A lovely vista

rite of offering beauty which had no price—such as the perfume of a wild flower. If there was a trifle to be eaten, she might serve it on a leaf, or in a wooden bowl—yet with elaborate ceremony, as though it were ambrosia in a chalice.

The other Byrdcliffe artists, less hermitically inclined, often assembled at the end of the day for an evening of stimulating conversation. It is doubtful if they enjoyed as much the Morris dances* in which Mrs. Whitehead expected them all to participate. She was a lady with a vision of the picturesque life remote from reality: one can imagine the effect upon the sweaty teamsters—struggling in the fields on a hot day—when she appeared in flowing gowns and veils, bearing a mead of non-fermented honey for their dubious refreshment! Though enjoying her romantically social life, she also treasured solitude, and was known to protect herself from uninvited guests by appearing at an upstairs window to call out, "Mrs. Whitehead is not at home."

Mr. Whitehead, more of a realist than she —but still very much an idealist himself— was joined in the initial planning and subsequent execution of his project by Hervey White and Bolton Brown. Brown had helped to choose the site for the colony, though he re-

---

* This was an old English dance of Moorish origin which became part of all village festivities in the reign of Henry VIII. It was usually danced by five men, together with a boy dressed in girl's habit and known as "Maid Marian." All wore gay costumes decorated with bells tuned to different notes so as to sound in harmony.

The joy of a keg . . . as opposed to a cup of unfermented honey

calls that when he and Whitehead met in Washington to consider his proposal, they discussed the fourth dimension over a steak dinner. In later years, Brown caused quite a stir with his remarks on democratic and majority rule. In an article for *The Plowshare*, a periodical published by Hervey White, he held that:

"Democracy does not favor art, science or education; the only freedom in a real democracy is the freedom to be like every other democrat. I recommend training the powers of the child and so to set its face, that it should try all things, that it therefore doubts all things, that it should get outside of mass hypnotism and see new truth—and perhaps God, in something else than its own class-image." (He slyly added: "But that, of course, would be for democracy to cut its own throat and cease to be a democracy.")

Hervey White, publisher of *The Plowshare* and other Woodstockian periodicals, was third in the triumvirate of artist-colony founders. He had a remarkable appearance, with his gray, ruffed-up hair, pointed beard and short smocks belted with scarves of contrasting colors. His clothes were home-dyed, faded purple, blue or magenta, and he wore them with inherent ease. His views on manual labor were similar to Whitehead's; he had written, while on a walking trip through Italy:

"As I live and learn I am getting the idea of the true dignity of work so thoroughly ingrained that I think I shall never feel it in me to write a tract about it; but instead, I shall during the rest of my life employ a good third of each day at some productive manual labor, seeing therein the only possible means of keeping a vigorous body, a healthy mind, and a conscience free towards my neighbor and myself."

It is interesting to compare this statement with that of Whitehead's. It seems inevitable that having met, the paths of these two men would merge; but it was also according to their natures that they could not travel for any length of time along a route together. For their pasts were antipathetic, though very much a part of each: Whitehead, the son of a wealthy merchant, had attended Oxford and later lived in a Florentine villa. White, a Kansas farm boy,

Hervey White ... Sometimes little children mistook him for Jesus Christ, and Hervey, a bit of an egotist, was usually reluctant to set them straight.

had worked his way through the State University, and then also traveled to Italy—but on a budget of thirty-five cents a day. Whitehead was used to order and discipline, and felt a measure of this necessary in a life of creative artistry; White emphatically did not. He moved from Byrdcliffe—to a section of land in the valley, saying:

A native farmer planting beans in the early days of Woodstock

The "Maverick horse," a symbol of the untamed, stood for many years at the entrance to the Maverick itself (see map). It was hewn by John Flanagan from a living tree—with the use of only an ax.

"One gets so tired of climbing a hill to get one's supper, it is better to live in the valley, and climb the hills for a view."

He chose to name his land "The Maverick," after a wild or untamed creature. While there, he set up a handpress, on which he printed his plays, books and magazines. In an early issue of *The Plowshare,* he wrote of Woodstock:

"Our special stock in trade is our humanness. We even include the institutions and conventions as essential to humanness. We are not revolutionaries; we are not the wild anarchists that onlookers might judge us from the freedom exhibited in our clothes. We are just ordinary nice people in the main . . . a little nicer than others it is true, but not so nice as to be devoid of interest and inspiration.

"Self-selected and of course well-selected."

"Woodstock is a group of idealists. . . . We are not all idealists however. That is the charming thing about Woodstock, that it isn't all of anything, nor yet quite all of everything. . . . On the whole we do not vastly differ from the denizens of the city. We are selected from the city, that is all. Self-selected and of course well selected."

Hervey's plays had few dramatic possibilities, but were interesting, nevertheless. In one, *The Woodcutter*, he spoke of "tree-feelings" and of the extraordinary peace and dignity which trees possess. In another, all the actors were to slide about on roller-skates, which would at least have been dramatic—if not absolutely fatal—

"Tree feelings" can be deeply sensed in John F. Carlson's dark-toned trunks and woodland shadows. Because of his great love of nature, perhaps Carlson, more than any other painter, firmly rooted his trees in the earth.
Sylvan Labyrinths
Painting by John F. Carlson

on the rickety little stage which he had had constructed. In later years, some very good theatre was played on the Maverick—with Helen Hayes, John Barrymore, and Edward G. Robinson among the various casts. Miss Hayes recalls a performance of Lady Gregory's *The Dragon*, for which she had to lie still in apparent death through nearly all of the final act. Mosquitoes began to settle in large groups for banqueting —she says it got so they didn't even fly away after a bite—just walked across to a fresh location. But she *did* keep still.

Through the years, the Maverick has also been noted for its concerts and festivals, with musicians from the Folies-Bergere, the Juilliard School, the Metropolitan Opera ... from Tanglewood, the Philharmonic, and various well-known orchestras all over the country.

In such a musical milieu did the *first* Woodstock Festival take place. Less widely publicized than some of the later variations on its theme (the media-saturated "happening" of August, 1969, is a notable example), this early fête was organized to finance the drilling of an artesian well. There had never been plumbing on the Maverick, but when even the water dipped by the pailful from the dug wells became scarce, Hervey reluctantly conceded that action must be taken. No water was found until the drill had bitten fifteen hundred feet into the Catskill rock and Hervey found himself fifteen hundred dollars in debt at a period when a dollar was worth a dollar. Hervey still more reluctantly conceded that *further* action must be taken, and so a festival was planned. On the date chosen, when the preparations were at last completed, it poured rain, as if the old squaw were laughing at all their efforts. It continued to rain for several days, and Hervey was in despair. Finally, to cheer him up, the musicians conspired to give him a tin pan serenade. They created such a clamor with buckets and dishpans that they must have frightened the old squaw into submission. The following day was clear. The sun,

followed by the moon, shone on the freshly-washed Catskills with invigorating purity.

The festival commenced with a short dramatic performance, after which the guests ate supper in a nearby meadow. Numerous bonfires were lighted, around which gathered gypsy-looking groups of people—cooking stews or toasting hot dogs, and boiling coffee in blackened pots. Everyone had tried to wear a costume, as the entrance fee was doubled for those who failed to appear in fancy dress—though this might be only a peasant smock and bright handkerchief around the head; or a wreath of grape leaves like the one Hervey wore to resemble Pan. Later the crowd, in their vivid array, took seats in the quarry—scambling to

Viewing the festival from points of vantage among the shelving rocks and "tailings" left by the stone-workers ... (Anita M. Smith is sketching)

points of vantage among the shelving rocks and "tailings" left by the stone-workers. Above them a white goat played along the rim, adding yet another decorative note to the sylvan scenery. A small orchestra played the works of Tchaikovsky, which resounded exquisitely from the walls of the rocky ampitheater. Darkness fell, but was gradually supplanted by the glow of a silver moon; then into its gentle light stepped a Russian dancer to present her recital. The music, the setting and the grace of her movements suffused her art in other—worldly beauty. It was, in short, one of those rare occasions when everything seemed perfect.

And it was this simple, lyrical beauty which Hervey valued above all. He often feared that the Maverick would be spoiled by the conveniences of a civilization he despised. He never realized that such beauty may be enhanced—and even ensured—by a degree of order and ease in the lives of those who help to create it. But basically he was right, for many of us would do well to clear from our lives those needless possessions, tangible or abstract, by which we are imprisoned. His opinion of property insurance was charmingly refreshing.

"If only one cottage burns every five years, I should end up better than if I'd paid to insure them."

He was referring to the several primitive cottages erected on the Maverick for the questionable comfort of resident actors and musicians. He himself finally shunned the confinement of even these most humble dwellings: his last months were spent in the midst of a locust thicket where, one evening, he peacefully died in his sleep. His funeral was simple, but very beautiful: musicians came from far and near to play his favorite chamber music in a hall decorated with boughs of flaming autumn maples. Several of Hervey's poems were read to his many friends that had come in tribute to a man who had brought much of art to Woodstock.

Hymn of Prayer

Tonight I come to Thee: ...
I ask not if Thou art, nor what nor where
I only come in faith, a yielding child:
I do not put the question "art Thou there?"
My morning's mood to see me would have smiled.
The day's full hours by wisdom were beguiled;
But now all closes in this humble prayer.

For loneliness is sweet, to Thee confessed:
For solitude is company with Thee;
Behind me fall ambitions richly dressed;
Before me love and trust of such degree
I have no thought of what success might be,
Or failure, for I rise reborn, reblessed.

One of the several poems by Hervey White which were read at his funeral service

Strange tales had come from the Maverick throughout the latter part of Hervey's life: of nudists, of bigamist relationships, *ménages à trois, quatre, cinq*—even of a man who believed he could acquire a mate by bellowing like a bull in the night ... and stranger still, he was said to have been successful!

Though these stories are rather amusing, and almost a natural phenomenon in groups like the one at Woodstock, they are often sources of irritation to the *real* artists who work very hard, and haven't the time for frequent partying and bizarrely impractical relationships.

Certainly the artists of Byrdcliffe and Rock City—an outgrowth to the east of the other— were a dedicated lot. They had to be, in order to survive. Though some of the Maverick actors and musicians were merely summer residents, the artists to the north braved the winter months, as well.

For many, the only shelters available were the barns in and around the Rock City area— so-called because of the slabs of quarried bluestone once piled there in readiness for shipment, or, simply because of the rocky soil. Levi Harder, who owned most of the barns, didn't think much of "pitcher paintin'," but he was

The Rock City "barnacle" dwellings

quick to see that it paid better to keep artists rather than hay or pigs in his buildings. Five dollars per month provided a studio for at least two "barnacles"—as the stable-dwellers were called—who would cut out windows in the upper half of the walls for a painting light. The villagers used to say that the only way to tell a studio from a chicken coop was to see if there were a window on the north side, which of course no respectable chicken would have tolerated.

For the winter months, one could purchase a pot-bellied stove, but this did little to temper

For the winter months, one could purchase a pot-bellied stove, but this did little to temper the icy winds. (John Carlson swore that when the belly of his stove was red hot he could pick icicles off its bottom.)

The prim path to a private plumbing housure

A Rock City Studio

the icy winds. Plumbing was of a chemical type, situated in a separate shed, and the cots, always nearer to the stoves than safety permitted, were a source of incredulity. One artist, in a fit of optimism, nicknamed hers "Gibraltar."

But none of these inconveniences seemed to quell the artists' enthusiasm. And many were lucky enough to take their meals with Mrs. Magee, a kindly soul who ran a boarding house at the corners.

Sandford and Rosie Magee had come to Rock City in order to look after Petrus Stroll, an aged and ailing farmer living on "The Corners." Petrus was a great one for cussing, and once, in years before, he'd sworn so hard over the stones which snagged his plow in the corn patch that he conjured up the Devil himself! The old demon promised to clear the field of stones if Petrus would deliver up his soul in a year's time. The angry farmer agreed, and for a season had no more trouble plowing. But the following spring when the Devil returned to claim his due, Petrus in a sassy mood just threw him the sole of his shoe. The Devil was in no mind to be cheated, however, and he returned not only the stones he had taken away, but twice as many more. Even today, that land is hopelessly filled with rocks.

Poor old Petrus was not the best of housekeepers, and had, apparently, little inclination

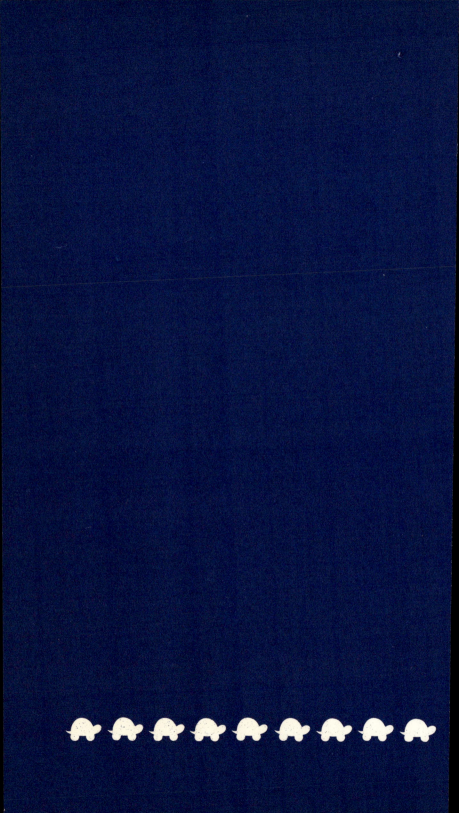

to cook. To save himself the trouble, he made a huge pile of pancakes every autumn which he set down-cellar in a crock of vinegar. Then every morning throughout the winter months, he would grab a few, rinse them off, and eat them for breakfast. He must have been very glad indeed when Rosie and Sandford came to "do" for him.

It was Rosie who really did the work. Sandford liked nothing better than to settle in his rocker and stroke his long, white beard, of which he was inordinately proud. One neighbor used to look across and say,

"There's Rosie's parlor ornament, a-settin' on the porch!" Rosie herself once cheerfully admitted that he was

"harder to get going than a British sloop!"

But Rosie took all the work in her stride— she virtually ran the farm *and* the boarding-house herself—and even found the time and money to indulge in treats for her animals. She bought box after box of shredded wheat and fed it to the chickens when she realized how much it meant to them.

She was especially kind to the artists. She gave them not only shredded wheat, but words of comfort, too. And doubtless she plied them with ample doses of the evil-smelling "skunk-fat" which she periodically "rended down" for her family's coughs and colds.

Eating at Rosie's was always an adventure: because she couldn't discipline her pets, one

Rosie Magee was seldom still except in the hundreds of sketches made of the Rock City corner. For in the days of Impressionist art in Woodstock the first enchanting sight of the crossroads always led the students to try painting a canvas. Approaching from Woodstock Village the composition seemed perfect. Through the branches of the old apple trees was the white house surrounded by a picket fence with splashes of red from a flowering shrub or the apples to match the color of the chimney. There was the hard-to-catch faded blue of Rosie's sunbonnet or the several layers of skirts, or the apron which usually held a few handfuls of grain to cast to the chickens which followed her about. Close to the house were weathered barns and sheds that shown warm gray against the blue of Overlook Mountain. The place was pictured through every season, from spring when the first cool greens crept over the valley under silver skies, to the full summer when the sun parched the grass and the mountain seemed to smoke in a heat wave. The students tried again in the autumn when the hard maples flamed in red and yellow against the brilliant blue of the sky that was usually painted as if scraps of denim had been stitched among the branches of the trees.
Old snapshot by Konrad Cramer

often had to brush a hen or kitten from one's place at the table. And it was wise to slice the butter thin, so as not to miss a feather. One obvious initiate chomped too heartily at a piece of delicious blueberry pie, and nearly broke his teeth on the shoe button nestled beneath the crust. Anne Moore, a neighborhood poetess at that time, caught a typical scene in "The Hen Came Clucking In":

> The hen came clucking in one day
> And found the chair.
> "I declare to goodness" said Rosie Magee,
> "If she ain't got Sweetie's place.
> I suppose I ought to drive her out,
> But it seems to fit her somehow.
> And Sweetie ain't wanting it just now."
> The hen stopped clucking long enough
> To lay an egg.
>
> "Well, it's nice anyway," said Rosie Magee,
> "To have her bring it here to me."

Miss Moore had a doctorate and several other degrees of higher learning; but it only made her laugh when, in later years, as she was working for Women's Suffrage, the digger of ditches whom she was trying to enlist in support of the Nineteenth Amendment looked up from his pick to say,

"What's the use of that? Wimen ain't edicated enough to vote!"

Andrew Dasburg is one of the many artists who remember Rosie with great affection.

Hercules (Herc) Davis, one-time beau of Rosie Magee . . . ("We sparked when we was young.")

"Mother Magee," he once wrote, "was even-tempered, hard-working—with a twinkle in her eye—and always greeted 'her boys' with a smile and a joking remark. 'Come Dasburg,' she would say, 'set down and eat your vittles.' Such breakfasts! All the eggs and bacon you could eat and sour-batter buckwheat cakes with maple syrup."

When for a while he lived in her house, she would often exclaim, "My souls alive, you're like a swingin' door, in and out of the house all day!"

Dasburg, a chief protagonist for the so-called "modern art," was by nature a revolutionist, ever hacking away at conservative painting and showing the way to fresh viewpoints—which had a wide impact on the other young artists. He had studied at the Art Students League in New York where he won a scholarship to come

Dasburg employed a modernistic but highly persuasive idiom in this, his powerful "Sermon on the Mount"

to Woodstock and work under Birge Harrison, for many years a resident instructor. Much as he liked Harrison personally, he was not happy painting in the subdued tones the older man recommended. He longed to express the brightness he saw around him; he and another student jokingly proposed a "sunflower club" in revolt against the moonlight formula. He began, increasingly, to experiment: one of his paintings created a sensation with its intriguing title, "The Absence of Mabel Dodge."

Woodstock was quickly gaining a reputation as an established center of art. Men like Robert Henri, George Bellows, and Rockwell Kent spent summers in Woodstock, and then, influenced by the pull of the mountain, often made their homes here.

George Bellows, perhaps the first great painter to be born, bred and nurtured exclusively in America, spent many hours with the younger artists in Woodstock:

"The student of art," he would say, "is continually at work both on art and on life. He gathers from the first what other minds have found, from the second he searches for new experiences. . . . The great school is where the great man teaches and where he finds students with heart enough and head enough to meet the ordeal. This truth implies the necessity on

An Art Students League class of 1913

the part of the student, however young, of becoming his own editor and judge of who and what for him is worthwhile.... Of what importance is art to society? All civilization and culture are the results of creative imagination or the artist quality in man. The artist is the man who makes life more interesting or beautiful, more understandable or mysterious, or probably in the last sense, more wonderful. His trade is to deal in illimitable experience. It is therefore only of importance that the artist discover whether he be an artist, and it is for society to discover what return it can make to the artist."

On a superficial level, society reacted to Bellows by giving him almost every available honor and prize. (He was, for example, the first ever to be given a one-man-show at the National Gallery in Washington.) The praise

was often effusive. In the Metropolitan Catalogue of the Bellows Memorial Show, a statement is made about the artist's well-known portrait of Mr. and Mrs. Philip Wase:

"Does it not put before us all that is left, in America, of Puritan austerity and rigour? How completely we are made to feel the discipline and self-denial, not only in the two people before us, but in thousands like unto them...."

The Rock City neighbors of Phil and Mrs. Wase would have been interested to read this. For though such paragons of virtue as the catalogue describes may have existed *someplace*, the Wases can not truthfully be counted among their ranks.

In fact, so lacking was Mr. Wase in that exquisite asceticism with which we are all so fond

George Bellows (lower left) with painters Andrew Dasburg and Charles Rosen at the baseball field

"... an' if we'd been-a-willin' to set without our clothes on we'd 'a' made twice as much..."
Mr. and Mrs. Phillip Wase
Painting by George Bellows

of crediting our forbears, that Mrs. Wase was often compelled to lock him in the bathroom when she went to do the village errands. But it is perhaps unfair to criticize, for certainly the pair showed commendable restraint in the affair of the portraiture. Mrs. Wase has been quoted as saying:

"Why you know we earned a dollar an hour just a-settin' there on the sofa in front of Mr. Bellows, an' if we'd been-a-willin' to set without our clothes on we'd 'a' made twice as much; but me, I won't let down my drawers for any artists!"

It is interesting to study the effect of the artists upon the natives of Woodstock. The reverse is obvious, for the influence of the coun-

Three of the more scintillating citizens of Woodstock

try people is made manifest in the actual creative work of writers, painters and performers. The antics of the "Cheats and Swings," a popular dancing group, were, for example, obviously borrowed from hill-billy mores.

But we catch a glimpse of the other in a story of the taxi driver who profited from the waits for customers by painting out of his taxi window, and who sometimes became so inspired in this activity that he refused to carry any but the most scintillating passengers. There was also the handy man who left his lawn-mowing half completed. When asked for an explanation he impatiently replied,

"Well I have to take some time to write if I'm to win the ten-thousand-dollar Atlantic Prize, now don't I?"

Some of the artists' Bohemianisms mildly startled their fellows; how must some of the more conservative members of the community

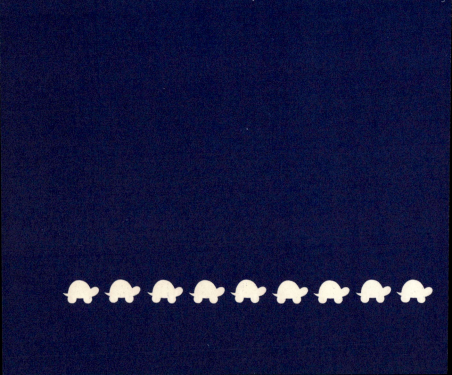

have greeted the male coiffures fashionable throughout the early twenties? For in Woodstock during this era, at least one man was seen with his head shaved to resemble a checkerboard; another's hair was cut in a series of polka-dots; and a third had the hair on the back of his head partially removed, leaving the outline of a face, with eyes, nose and mouth.

But if many of the natives were often surprised and even outraged at the artists' "goings-on," the more tolerant conceded that the artists could also be very kind. It was, for example, Clara Chichester, a pianist, who discovered and gave to Rosie Magee the thing she'd wanted all her life: a pair of pink satin slippers . . . to be buried in.

But even more important, the artists saved the villagers from the hideous fate of boredom. Ennui has never flourished in Woodstock—a fact due, at least in part, to the wild rumors and shocking tales which continually flow from the artists' encampments. Perhaps it is true that "ordinary people" are guilty of just as many indiscretions, but haven't the weakness—or the flair—for widespread publicity.

And certainly, the artists have, through the years, fallen prey to their own talent for exaggeration. Their parties have been neither as numerous or as scandalous as they may have

seemed to be; and some of the most fascinating have been extraordinarily decorous. One such was a dinner party at which the host (a Dr. Kingsbury) served different mushrooms for every course, and at one point extinguished the lights so that his guests might eat solely by the phosphorescent glow of their culinary fungus.

An expert on edible mushrooms, Dr. Kingsbury had also made a study of astronomy, and so often gave "star parties" as well. A friend recalls that at one of these "a talk was given by the head of the Hayden Planetarium . . . and during a special Perseid shower, the constellation Perseus was outlined by candles anchored in the swimming pool. . . ."
The invitation (above) was the one sent out for this particular party.

At many of their parties the artists have been too deeply involved in discussions of Art itself to need to resort to sensational behavior. And of course the more dedicated artists have rarely attended parties at all—they have come to Woodstock not for "the action," nor on a parasitic quest for excitement, but for the freedom to pursue their work—that being the business of creativity.

The Italian sculptor, Alfeo Faggi, had a theory that climate and background are responsible for the encouragement or deterioration of the artistic impulse. He cites Florence, Paris and *Woodstock* as places where creative imagination is stimulated.

Once, while studying an early Michelangelo sculpture at the Casa Buonarroti, a guard told him that "the master said the artist ought not to copy things as they are but as they should be. Thus we have, from the lips of an elderly caretaker a revelation of the true field of art, and one for which Woodstock has seemingly been an inspiration—the realm of imagination.

Faggi has told a charming story, in which he befriended a cat and later invited him home. He observed that the cat had one eye open, the other closed, one ear up and the other down. Looking carefully at his friend, Faggi saw the cat to be more intelligent than himself. However, he said to him:

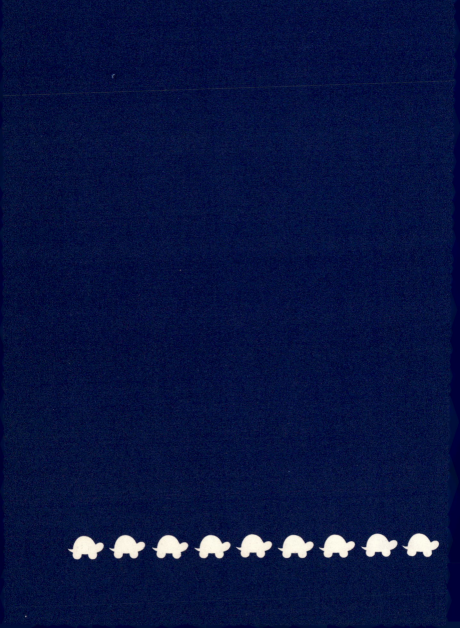

Alfeo Faggi cast in bronze these scenes from the life of another who talked with animals and birds, St. Francis of Assisi.

"I not like fleas and though I don't see any fleas maybe you have them, so I feed you, but you must sleep outside on the porch. 'Yes,' the cat replied.

"He stay round for several days and I make drawings of that cat, and then the cat he say, 'You not artist but a business man. I go away now.' Soon he disappear and I never see him again, but I sell all those drawings and he was right: I do business from that cat!"

There are many stories from the mountains surrounding Woodstock of animal wisdom and intelligence. If ony we, like Faggi, would listen to their counsel. . . .

From the mountains too, have come stories of witches. . . .

For those piglets who survived the terrors of witchery...

It is said that the witch of Sugarloaf Mountain coveted one of her neighbor's piglets. When the farmer refused to give it up, the wicked woman was so enraged she bewitched the entire litter, as a result of which they would do nothing but dance on their noses. The farmer, realizing what had befallen his pigs, was obliged to cut off their curly tails and throw them into a fire. This cured the pigs, who immediately ceased their ignominious dancing, but it did, predictably, injure the

. . . there was the adult ordeal of the pig-scalding.

witch. She was found scratching in the farmer's fireplace, trying to salvage the charred remains of the piglet tails, but she only succeeded in badly burning her foot. Thereafter she limped about with one misshapen limb, upon which she wore three socks. She was not at all deterred by the encounter, but continued to employ—and proudly boast—her witchly powers. She had special magic words she used such as "Pocks E' Rollins," and whoever heard her say them was certain to fall upon evil luck—unless, of course, the victim quickly consulted a reputable witch doctor.

Depending upon the diagnosis, the latter would issue various cathartics and carminatives as well as a generous portion of "mumbo jumbo."

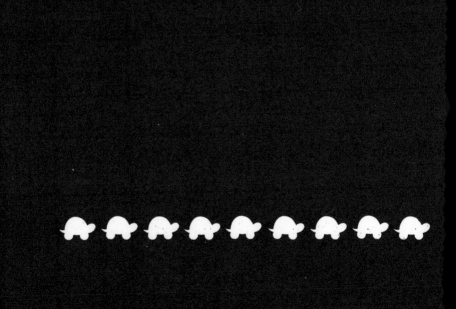

Old Doc Brink of Lake Katrine, a favorite practitioner, was especially noted for his wondrous "eyewash," which he kept in a hand blown bottle and made from the purest waters of the last snowfall of the previous winter.

The mountain people were grateful for the presence of these "doctors," for they were often puzzled and a little frightened by the inexplicable phenomena they found in their daily lives. Who can explain, for example, the waters that suddenly burbled forth on moonlit nights in the midst of extended droughts. "Yes," said a lady, shaking her head, "I've seen it happen to the spring at the back of this very house. All at once it will rise and overflow for no reason we can see, unless it's the pull of the moon." Should we thus concur with the farmer who insists, "There are tides in the mountains as well as in the sea"?

"There are tides in the mountains as well as in the sea."

Whatever the answer, none may doubt that there *is* a power in this community of Woodstock: whether it comes from the moon, from the mountains themselves or from a greater force as yet unexplained, it has shaped a place of rare beauty and creativity.

Woodstock has been a home of the Indians, and a dwelling of their God . . . as later it became a refuge for the settlers of many different origins. It has been a home to glassblowers, to quarrymen and tanners . . . to farmers (to "Rickety Ricks" and "Bide Snyder") . . . to poets, philosophers, physicians and musicians, to writers and painters, to weavers and potters —and yes, to butchers and bakers and Whisper-Fan-makers.* . . .

It is a place of beast and flower, of tree and stone:
of linx 'n fox 'n sturdy oxen,
of daisies and devil's paintbrush,
of great forests . . .
of occasional ledges providing scanty foothold for a spruce or scrub oak which spreads its crooked arms t' leeward.
(To the mountain people, these were not trees, but ancient crones, chained to the rocks in merited retribution for sins untold but terrible.)

---

* Rotron Incorporated, a creator of cooling devices, has flourished in Woodstock for many years.

With her crooked arms t' leeward
Painting by Henry Mattson

It is a place of mystery and legend, of wonder and inspiration.

It is Woodstock, the child of one force and master of another. . . .

And that power is one generated by many years of creative effort. For nothing is ever lost. Since the birth of the Woodstock Nation—not the one which began with the Rock and Ston-ed Festival of 1969 (though this also has its place), but instead, with the Byrdcliffe colony of the early nineteen hundreds—since the advent of this nation (with its heritage even unto the Amerindian) the dominant thinking in Woodstock has been toward higher ideals in art. Some may die without achieving tangible success, but every thought lives on and serves to lift another generation's ambition toward perfection.

WOODSTOCK: A Nostalgic Portrait

A New Yorker's View of the Woodstock Maverick Festival of 1915

How picture this glamorous convention? How find words of adequate relish to describe its vivid delights? Few would readily credit a village in the Catskills with so much of raciness, flavor and "folk," such potentiality for sparkling revelry and indigenous wit. In all its kaleidoscopic aspects, the (Woodstock) Maverick Festival is greatly alluring. . . .

A glade, a clearing, a natural amphitheatre and impending forests, on the night of the full moon in August! From early afternoon people in costumes commence to foregather from miles around, lords and ladies on horseback, gypsies in their caravans, Indians in war paint,

Off for the Maverick

Anita M. Smith as an emigrant

clowns and buffoons in ornate motor cars, peasants of all nations, kings, queens and princesses of all epochs, humans of all generations at present extant "with all the paraphernalia of simplicity," the more enterprising revellers erecting merry-go-rounds, booths and treehuts, and all alike building in the open space bonfires, whereon to prepare the evening meal, and whereby to await the night's entertainments.... At dusk the company is well assembled, more romantic than legend, more splendid than Arabia....
Alexander Brook
New York: June, 1923*

---
* This material has been quoted from Alexander Brook's "The Woodstock Whirl," an article which appeared in *The Arts* magazine of that month and year.

Gypsies in their caravans

The more enterprising revellers

More romantic than legend, more splendid than Arabia

WOODSTOCK: A Psychic Portrait

A Londoner's View of the Woodstock Music Festival of 1969

In the Springtime of the new Aquarian Age WOODSTOCK was the first vibration to be sent out from the North American continent. It made the first great rift in the still closely encircling clouds that yet linger as we are just beginning to emerge from the dark Cycle of Kali.

WOODSTOCK — poised mid-air between two decades—defined in dramatic occurrence an extraordinary psychic summation. In swift, cantilever fashion, this new vibration spiraled up from the apparatus-oriented sixties. It was a vibration of anarchical creativity—fostering music, love, and peace as mates of play... and thereby increasing inter-connectiveness in youth.

Lesser festivals than THE ONE of August 1969 have occurred all the way from Magic Mountain to Monterey. It is argued that the smaller events are of more significance. They are more congenial, less mind-blowing. But inevitably their yardstick is WOODSTOCK.

And thus it is that knitted neatly into the archives of our memories resides the experience which was WOODSTOCK. Strident calls have gone out, in the intervening years, promising greater "happenings"—or, threatening

greater disasters, according to smug citizenry barb. Time and perspective, however, have dimensionally outflanked all others—so that one must lie content with dream and memory. For as songs, plays and films are able to record, within time, the echo of an age, so WOODSTOCK, poised mid-air--

Crossing the currents of time the flower people were but a fading vision: a congregation of youth floating on the day to day. . . . Eked or limitless pennies providing the sustenance, the mobility of the thought was helped to gestation. Indeed, such was the potency, that nearly half a million made it and another half was prevented from doing so only by the sheer effluence which choked the arteries of White Lake, Town of Bethel,* New York. Spinning symmetrically from the metropolis since May on the waves of WABC (there *were* other stations, I believe) came numberless dispatches. Underground and over ground the ceaseless patter grew, developed, and magnetized the hearers. Interest spiraled: in three days one could see more highlights than Bill Graham could roll together in as many months.

Not bad. Meanwhile the animal was finding it difficult to lie down. So big had it become that

---

* In our limited spatial sense White Lake in the Township of Bethel, New York (where the Festival finally occurred) seems some little distance from the community of Woodstock. But in cosmic terms, though based in another village, the Festival . . . Happened in Woodstock.

it must have looked similar to the one George Wein was hoping to tie up.* Thus the township of Woodstock faced the beast and railroaded it out of town.

Next came Wallkill. It seemed as though the site had been found. At least the scaffolding started to go up, but perhaps this was only because of the desperate shortage of time. Now, fully more beast than corporation, the giant stumbled westward and before the farmers of Bethel, New York—who were understandably not spiritual engineers—could wholeheartedly grant their consent, they were enveloped. By that time it is doubtful whether any community could have stemmed the onslaught of the incalculable energy and magnetism through which a common mind was channeling itself.

And then the event itself emerged—from the barest routing outline—heaving and choking in the massive swell which crested at Exit 16 on the New York Thruway. Soon the air waves were crowded with the "disaster." Local radio stations warned of the hopeless mess and told dire tales. A common goal, however, brought compatibility, whereas those of older mind or different vibratory rate could only launch attacks. Then it rained. Now it really was a mess. But out of this natural cooling process evolved the spirit which was to hold the

---

* In 1964 Mr. Wein—of Newport Jazz fame—attempted to transplant that festival to Woodstock.

event together and to be the proof of its significance to youth itself. Foreboding words evoked laughter—and against laughter there is no defence. As the words of the damning soothsayers turned to ashes, the community began to get down to the chore of enjoying itself and helping the other guy.

Briefly, the protracted struggle and unending hassles were eclipsed; and people could act naturally in order to gain their ends. Bedrooms, living rooms and kitchens were moved to the outdoors in convoluted form. And baring what was innermost and soaking in what was denied, the natural way was opened and became operative as the group's soul met under the skies in the natural amphitheatre provided by Max Yasgur. Sending the bauble that eyed them ever higher were the cream of the crop.** No matter where one sat ... or stood ... or lay ... one could at least occasionally catch their cybernetic beat—and at other times the wind discretely blew heavenwards. In the months after some of the groups would believe too much in the part that they played and thus lose their context in the event. Others neatly packaged their experience, and they, like the participants, hoped that something would happen similarly ... some day ... somewhere.

Thus for a moment the organized community was forced to rely on faith. Within the arena

---

** See page 165

the local residents did what they could with their culinary skills and seemed to enjoy the unexpected. Most certainly, the spirit of the Hog Farm—as well as that of many individuals—cannot be forgotten, and this spirit helps to explain the significance of what was happening in the sixties. . . . But more—the event was a breaking out—an expression of the elements of nature: Color, Smell and Sound were there. And when Color, Smell and Sound are allowed to combine with a highly motivated energy moving toward a goal adamantly desired by all, a final expression will not be denied.

I very much doubt whether there ever could be a situational similarity: even the outsiders, powerless, participated—as the soul of the future was allowed to emerge, intermingle and play an increasingly expansive, prancing Pan. But let us hope—as earth cycles through the seventies—for a time when the awakening spirit of the sixties, which culminated at the Woodstock Music Festival, will be self-operative —leaving humans free to pursue a tri-fold unity of body, mind and spirit as we sweep onward and upward in an ever ascending spiral. . . .

London: June, 1971

© 1972 Stonecrop

WOODSTOCK: An Addendum

THE MAVERICK FESTIVAL
August 30th, 1929

(If rainy, the next fair day, save Sunday)

PROGRAM OF THE DAY

4:00	P. M.	Grounds Open.
4:30	"	Music by Mink Hollow Fiddlers—Free Dancing.
5:00	"	Games Acrobatics, Sports, Strolling Musicians and Players.
7:00	"	Camp-fire Suppers.
9:00	"	Open Air Theatre Performance, "THE GAY NINETIES."
10:40	"	Torchlight Procession.
10:45	"	DANCE IN PAVILLION—Costume Ball—Open Air Dance of Country Dances (three dancing platforms).

Full program of "THE GAY NINETIES" on opposite page.

DELICIOUS MEALS

JUDY'S

ORDERS TAKEN FOR

MAVERICK FESTIVAL

Meat Pies
Fruit Tarts
Baked Spaghetti, etc.

Picnic Baskets to Order

MATERIAL AND MAKE-UP
FOR MAVERICK FESTIVAL
Now on Sale at
The Little Art shop, Woodstock, N.Y.

"THE GAY NINETIES"

Given at the

Maverick Open Air Theatre

for the

ANNUAL MAVERICK FESTIVAL
9:00 P. M.

Program of Performance

A Procession of Celebrities of the Period.

E. Tanner, Song.

Mink Hollow Ball.

Bessie Pendleton, Country Jig.

Floradora Sextette, Ruth Schrader and the Schrader Dancers.

Midway Pleasaunce Dancers.

Cake Walk

Negro Spirituals and Tap Dance, Dolly and Jack La Tour.

Alexis Kosloff's Ballet (featuring Marguerita Gakinoff, Priscilla Baker, Mary D. DuFrey, Fritzie DuFrey, Betty Wood, Nan Reasoner, Alice Westervelt and Elsie Harriman) La Nuit, Rubenstein.

Sullivan and Corbett Fight.

Belbridge's Bathing Beauties.

Ruth Schrader's Serpentine Dance.

Felix's Fancies, classical ballet.

After the Ball, grand finale.

For this performance there will be two bands, Georges Barrere's Classical Band and Ernie's Jazz Band.

These celebrities of the day will be on the stage: Anna Held, Wm. Jennings Bryan, P. T. Barnum, Lillian Russell, Eva Tangway, John L. Sullivan, Terry McGovern, Young Corbett, Buffalo Bill, Sitting Bull, John Philip Sousa, Professor Ernie.

Fountain effects by Ned Thatcher; pageant direction, Walter Steinhilber.

LONGYEAR BUS LINES
TOURING AND TAXI SERVICE
WOODSTOCK, N. Y.

| WILLOW | LAKE HILL | SHADY | BEARSVILLE |
| WOODSTOCK | WEST HURLEY | | KINGSTON |

For any of the above places, go to Kingston's uptown Bus Terminal; then take Longyear's Buses

From Woodstock take Longyear's Buses to the Maverick Theatre and Concerts and to the Phoenix Theatre

Longyear's touring cars and taxi service for any other points off the bus lines

Ship trunks, baggage and express to Woodstock care of Longyear's Express. No storage charges. Special attention given to your baggage and express shipments out or in the Woodstock valley

Send for bus schedule or telephone 16 Woodstock

ICE-CREAM SODA

STATIONERY
ART SUPPLIES
DANDY KANDY

The Nook

WOODSTOCK-N.Y.

Hot Plate Dinner 75c

Always Ready and a la Carte

Open Evenings for Small Parties.

RADIO FOR DANCING
Waffles - Coffee - Ice Cream
WOODSTOCK-SAUGERTIES ROAD

The Jack Horner Tea Room

Breakfast   *Luncheon*

Tea   *Dinner*

WOODSTOCK, N. Y.

Mme. Anna E. Ziegler
Voice Teacher

Metropolitan Opera House
New York

Summer Season
at Woodstock

PING PONG PARLOR
WOODSTOCK VALLEY HOTEL
Come and See Woodstock's
Latest Racquet
JOE MAGLEY, Professional

AN ARTIST'S HOME
FOR SALE
In Wittenburg Valley

10-room house, 2 sleeping porches, 2 baths, gravity water, separate studio in barn, 36 acres of land, apple, plum, peach and cherry trees.

SACRIFICE!
Call for Appointment
WOODSTOCK 11-F-5.

H. B. MERRITT

413-415 Washington Avenue

Tel. 1188.   KINGSTON, N. Y.

A Few of Our
BARGAIN PRICES
For the Coming Week

Legs of Lamb	32c
Lamb Chops	25c
Loin of Lamb	28c
Chuck Pot Roast	20c
Bacon	17c
Fowls	25c
Turkeys	45c
Flour, sack	85c
Eggs, 3 dozen	$1.00
Regular Ham	25c
Fresh Mackerel	19c
Butter, 2 lbs.	67c
Evap. Milk, 3 for	23c
200 Chesterfield Cigarettes	$1.00
200 Old Gold Cigarettes	$1.00
Sugar, cwt.	$4.69
3 lbs. Coffee	57c

Woodstockers Like to Shop With Us!

Club Breakfasts
25c to 75c
Luncheon
50c and $1.00
Dinner, $1.00
Including
Sundays

Fine Bakery
Products
at
Twin Gables
Bake Shop

VISIT OUR RAINBOW GARDENS FOR LUNCHEON AND TEA

A. J. Daiber   10th Year   Tel. 159

HIKING TOURS

over little known Catskill Mountain trails —conducted by Dyrus and Edith Cook. Five-day trips. Small parties. Comfortable beds in the open. Campfire cooking. Pack animal for toting. Write for particulars. Box 353, Woodstock, N. Y.

PING PONG PARLOR
NOW SITUATED BEHIND THE NOOK
JOE MABLEY, Professional
Woodstock's Only Night Club

Sodas & Fine Candies
Kodaks, Gifts
Dry Goods
Art Supplies
Picture Framing
Stationery
Printing and
Developing

The Little Art Shop
WOODSTOCK, N. Y.

WATSON HOLLOW INN
OVERLOOKING THE FAMOUS ASHOKAN

A unique place to dine in the open, where porches look out upon the lake and "the misty mountain winds are free to blow against thee."

Dinner and Luncheon served from 12 M to 7:30 P.M.
Refreshments 12 M to 11 P.M.

DANCING IN THE PUMPKIM ROOM
Every Tuesday Evening 8 To 12.
LADY AND GENTLEMAN $1.00
The Regular Dinner Will Include Dancing.

Music by Maisenhelder's Orchestra.

Accommodations for tourists.
For reservations, address: Watson Hollow Inn, West Shokan,
New York—Phone— Shokan 9-F 12

CHARACTER IS DESTINY
EDITH HARLAN
Astrologist
Specialist in Astro-psycho-analysis and Horary Charts.
Classes and Lectures by Arrangement

EASTON FARM

Woodstock, N. Y.   -:-   Phone 4-F-22

Horoscopes Read

RITZ-ALLEN RESTAURANT
WOODSTOCK, NEW YORK
Telephone Woodstock 103

MENU

Olives   Radishes   Celery
Soup
Chicken with Rice
Roast
Vermont Young Turkey
Ham, Dressing, Currant Jelly
Vegetables
Green Peas   Mashed Potatoes
Salad
Combination, French Dressing
Dessert
Strawberries with Fresh Cream   Rice Pudding
Tea, Coffee or Milk

Keeney's Theatre

Monday, Tuesday, Wednesday and Thursday
AUGUST 1, 2, 3, 4
TOM MIX in "THE TROUBLE SHOOTER"

Friday and Saturday
AUGUST 5, 6
BETTY COMPSON in "THE ENEMY SEX"

THE OLD WOODSTOCK INN
"ON THE GREEN"

As Homelike As Possible Away From Home

Two stately maples guard its ancient walls, and form an arch of green. And there appear a multitude- -a thousand several souls, to breathe its atmosphere.

Telephone Woodstock 78

ACCOMODATIONS BY DAY OR WEEK

WOODSTOCK, N. Y.

DANCING CLASSES

ALEXIS KOSLOFF

Of the Metropolitan Opera House, New York City

Formerly of the Imperial Russian Ballet

Dancing Classes in the Maverick Theatre During June, July, August and September

ADULT CLASSES	SPECIAL CHILDREN'S CLASSES
INTERPRETIVE, CLASSIC, ECCENTRIC, CHARACTER, PANTOMIME, PLASTIQUE	SOLO DANCES GROUP DANCES BAR EXERCISES

STAGE AND TOE DANCING AND FENCING

PRIVATE LESSONS BY APPOINTMENT
MAKE RESERVATIONS FOR THE 1930 SEASON.

Enquire at MR. KOSLOFF'S ESTATE
Maverick Road, Woodstock, N. Y.

PICTURES

at Firemen's Hall

Woodstock

The Home of the Best Made Pictures

MONDAY

Thomas Meighan in his latest release

TONGUES OF FLAME

No picture Tuesday owing to the dance for Joan of Arc Church

WEDNESDAY

Watch for our advertising on Wednesday's picture

Good order is always maintained in our Theatre

FRIDAY

The Big Special

NORTH OF 36

Better than the Covered Wagon

Watch the Hue and Cry for our weekly program

SATURDAY

FIGHTING FURY

starring Jack Hoxie

A Western—full of thrills

COMING

C. B. DeMille production, The Golden Bed

This is his latest production

Knife and Fork Restaurant

WOODSTOCK, N. Y.

Breakfast -:- Lunch
Dinner

**Sandwiches, Salads, Ice Cream and Pies
are served until midnight**

Outdoor Tables, Facing the Village Green.

Picture Credits and Acknowledgments

vii   Cover of *The Woodstock Bulletin*, circa 1930; artist unknown

x   Cover of *Woodstock*, a Woodstock Chamber of Commerce publication issued circa 1930; artist unknown

13   Cover of *The Woodstock Bulletin*, March 15, 1930; Pamela V. Brown

19   *The Woodstock Press*

23   Courtesy of *The New York Times*

29   Photograph by L. E. Jones

33   "Mountain Valley," a painting by Ethel Magafan

37   Postcard by L. E. Jones

47   Photograph by Konrad Cramer

51   Photograph owned by Mrs. Olney Cooke

55   Photograph by Konrad Cramer

59   "Snow-mantled Highways," a painting by John F. Carlson

71   Cover of *The Woodstock Bulletin*, September 1, 1929; Pamela V. Brown

77   "Sylvan Labyrinths," a painting by John F. Carlson

89   "Rock City View," a painting by Lucille Blanch

97   Snapshot by Konrad Cramer

111   "Mr. and Mrs. Philip Wase," a painting by George Bellows

121   Scenes from Life of St. Francis (bronze relief) by Alfeo Faggi; Art Institute of Chicago

131   Painting by Henry Mattson

With special thanks to Aileen Cramer and Margot (Cramer) Taylor for permission to use their father, Konrad's, photographs.

Cream of the Crop

Joan Baez
The Band
Blood, Sweat and Tears
Paul Butterfield Blues Band
Canned Heat
Joe Cocker
Country Joe and the Fish
Creedence Clearwater Revival
Crosby, Stills, Nash and Young
Grateful Dead
Arlo Guthrie
Tim Hardin
Keef Hartley
Richie Havens
Jimi Hendrix
Incredible String Band
Jefferson Airplane
Janis Joplin
Melanie
Mountain
Santana
John Sebastian
Sha-na-na
Ravi Shankar
Sly and the Family Stone
Bert Sommer
Sweetwater
Ten Years After
The Who
Johnny Winter

Cover photograph of Hervey White by Konrad Cramer

Printed in U.S.A.